365 Relationship Quotes For Women

By Allan Wesley

Effective Relationship Advice for Women

About this book:

I wrote this book primarily because of the overwhelmingly positive responses to my Facebook quotes. I wrote it for you – women. I call it "365 Relationship Quotes for Women" since there are 365 days in the year there is a quote for each day. The quotes are really advice that you can read daily for whatever relationship aliment you might have or to help guide you through or prevent a relationship aliment – divorce, loneliness, insecurities, deception, a third party in the relationship, unhappiness, feeling unappreciated, being taken for granted, men, sex, etc...

I hope that some of these quotes become your mantras of sorts to aid you through difficult times and to help prevent difficult ones arising. You can and you should read some of them back to a man as appropriate. The quotes contained herein are all my original thoughts. They are very practical, powerful and candid. I have avoided "dressing up" these quotes because when you need relationship advice, you, in my opinion, don't need words wrapped or clothed in Shakespearean type language. You need to hear plain simple advice or words to which you can immediately relate. For example, if you are looking for love, I'm not sure you want to hear me tell you, "Love is like an endless blooming flower watered by the perpetual pouring of the warm feelings of two hearts." Sure, this quote sounds wonderful but how practical is it? How does it help you as compared to "Look for a man who also loves you"? If you can't find or you don't seek a man who also loves you, you won't be able to fully appreciate the first quote. I deal with practicality and so should you in your relationships. You can read this book in any order since there's no particular reading order to the book. Every 5th day, I've chosen to expand on the quote. Therefore days 5, 10, 15, 20, etc... have expanded quotes. Most of the quotes, I believe, are self-explanatory. However, I've had requests before to explain the meaning of a particular quote. Hence, I thought it would be beneficial to give you more to read by expanding on every fifth quote.

Happy reading, and please, even though these quotes are deliberately not lengthy, they do pack a powerful punch. Don't only read them but heed them as well. They are most effective when heeded.

Day 1

Avoid men who are visible for sex but invisible for everything else.

Day 2

Never want a man so badly that you are willing to change who you are just to have him.

Day 3

Don't approach relationships with the mindset of, "I am lonely and I need someone." The better mindset is, "I want someone who is deserving of me."

Day 4

When someone loves and cares about you, you don't have to second-guess their actions.

Day 5

It's not a real relationship if the man is physically there but emotionally absent — he's just there.

Having a man be physically with you is very different from having a man who is also emotionally there for you, unless all you are looking for is a physical relationship. There is no shortage of men physically swooning over you and that will always be the case. A man's willing emotional involvement with you signifies a relationship, a commitment. Having a man be there for you emotionally means, amongst other things, having a man whom you can comfortably talk to about any and everything. It means having a man you can turn to and rely on when the chips are down, a man who is a true companion with whom to have conversations, share outings, laughs and life's many happy and sad moments. Providing support to help you through life's roller coaster of emotions is not the same as a mere physical presence. Physical presence does not guarantee emotional support. Hence a man should be both physically and emotionally there for you.

Day 6

If you keep having failed relationships take refuge in being single for a while, it's the one relationship that won't fail you.

Day 7

The right man for you is the man to whom you never told your expectations but he met or exceeded them all.

Day 8

Real men don't try to lift themselves up by putting you down.

Day 9

Sometimes a man is worth the wait but only if he has demonstrated that he wants you just as much or even more than you want him.

Day 10

If you lower your value to attract men, you will attract men of low value.

You hold yourself to a high standard and of this you should be proud. That you are single or that men don't seem to swarm all over you should not be the impetus for you to lower your standards. The right man who fulfills those high standards you have set for yourself—and for him—will eventually come along. Why should you lower your standards or expectations of men in order to attract or get a man? I'm sure your standards and expectations do not include a man with wings. The point being that there is someone who will meet and even exceed your expectations. Remember, just as you have set high standards and expectations, there are men out there who have also set high expectations to meet a woman like you. It just has not happened yet.

Day 11

Some men were meant to be friends only—no benefits.

Day 12

Not having a man does not make you any less of a woman.

Day 13

Every man is not the one, only one man is.

Day 14

It's not about the men that are attracted to you; it's about the men you choose – so choose carefully.

Day 15

You can't keep falling for the same tricks, lies and empty promises and blame it all on the man.

Okay, so he lied and charmed his way into your heart or maybe even just got you into bed, then he vanished or the relationship (assuming one developed) didn't work out. Again, you entered into a relationship and yet again, sadly, it didn't work out. Being a romantic or wanting to be loved, you tried yet again. You entered another relationship and that also didn't last. If you keep on having failed relationships, you should take a break from getting into one and examine the reasons for the past failures. Sometimes, it's not the man. Sometimes it's just you and you have to be honest with yourself. You have to analyze your past relationships and see what mistakes you have made or are making, because it would seem that you are making some mistakes. Ask questions of yourself and of the relationship. The hope is that you will learn from your mistakes and apply those lessons to your next relationship to improve your chances of being in a lasting one.

Day 16

If you gave him a second chance but he needs a third maybe you need to give yourself a chance to be alone.

Day 17

If someone says, "I love you" on the first date, then someone is lying.

Day 18

As a woman you are priceless, so don't allow a man to put a price on you.

Day 19

The women who get along best with men are the women who can get along without them. Are you that type of woman?

Day 20

Some relationships were not meant to be because you were meant to be with someone else.

Not all relationships were meant to be and this is primarily based upon how the relationship started and the individual with whom you entered into the relationship. Some relationships were rushed, forced, experimental, rebounds, etc... which you entered into even though you knew that 'friends' would have been a better categorization or labeling of the relationship. In some instances, there was nothing in common or only a few things and yet the relationship was started. And in other cases, it commenced purely out of a physical attraction or interaction. When such a relationship ends, it really is "a blessing in disguise," to use that old cliché. Sometimes, two people really weren't meant to be with each other and this becomes obvious the longer they remain together. If this is scenario applies to you, the sooner you realize it, the sooner you can move on and find the person meant for you. Don't force a relationship.

Day 21

Never let others pressure you into a relationship and never pressure yourself to get into one.

Day 22

Understand that a man in your bed is not the same as a man in your life.

Day 23

It's better to be by yourself until you find someone you can be yourself with – someone who loves you for you.

Day 24

Good sex alone will not keep him. It may keep him coming back, but only for sex, not for you.

Day 25

The most expensive gift a man can give you is unconditional love – it's priceless.

Most of you would probably not refuse expensive gifts of jewelry, cars, homes, vacations, etc... However, those things are material in nature. You could have all that and still have an emotional void that not even the most expensive of gifts can fill. If you have everything except the true love of a man, then it's possible you are still an unhappy woman. I'm talking to women who want a relationship. There is no price tag on the feeling of knowing someone loves you unconditionally, someone who demonstrates such – no judgments, loves you the way you are, you don't have to change for him and you experience this love daily. Such a gift of unconditional love makes all others pale in comparison.

Day 26

He should know that simplicity speaks volumes - a call, text, card, flowers and small gestures.

Day 27

Don't tell me you love me, show me.

Day 28

A real woman does not compete with other women for a man; she is confident in who she is and knows what she wants.

Day 29

He can only play games if he has someone to play them with; don't be his playmate.

Day 30

Want a great relationship? Start with someone who also wants you for the right reasons.

We can't predict how a relationship will turn out – how long it will last, will it end in marriage, will he change, will you change your views on the relationship, etc... Predictability aside, a great start to a relationship and a foundation on which to build is to choose someone who also wants to be with you for the right reasons. It's the perfect beginning for a great relationship and it increases the possibility of you having a lasting relationship. Too often, people enter into relationships too quickly and for the wrong reasons. Make sure he wants you as much as you want him and not because he said so but because he shows you daily.

Day 31

Sex is not love.

Day 32

Cheating men are a part of life but they do not have to be a part of yours – unless you want them to be.

Day 33

It's not selfish to want to be happy; it's selfish not to want to compromise.

Day 34

Men are not perfect, but it would be perfect if they were truthful to women about what they really want.

Day 35

Single woman prayer – Lord, grant me the man you know I deserve.

Never be afraid of being single. Never view single as a stigma. Never be rushed from your single status into a relationships status. Wait and look for the man you know you deserve. Sadly, there are many women who are in relationships but are still lonely. Their status reads, "In a relationship" but in their hearts they are lonely. This is the situation you must seek to avoid; it's better to be single and lonely than be lonely in a relationship. Be patient and wait for the man know you deserve.

Day 36

Even a doormat gets worn out after being repeatedly stepped on. The difference between you and a doormat – choice.

Day 37

Sometimes your happiness is just a breakup away.

Day 38

His looks can draw you in but his behavior and personality could push you away.

Day 39

Sometimes, it's not that he cheated on you, it's that you cheated yourself by getting into a relationship with him.

Day 40

Only a fool gets into a relationship just to say that they are in one.

Some people take keeping up with the Jones' too far. Having the latest high tech device, driving an expensive car and wearing only designer brand clothing may be trendy or fashionable. Being in a relationship is neither trendy nor fashionable. The fact that all of your friends are in relationships, hopefully happy ones, does not mean that you have to literally run out there and get into one too. Such thinking and acting is asinine. You get into a relationship when you've met someone who also genuinely wants to get into one with you. It's better to not be in a relationship than to be in a bad one.

Day 41

It's not easy closing your heart to someone for whom it was always open but sometimes he leaves you with no other choice.

Day 42

If one person is unhappy in the relationship, then it's an unhappy relationship.

Day 43

She didn't break up your relationship by herself; she had help – your man.

Day 44

Sometimes, at the ending of a relationship, you see the things you should have seen from the beginning.

Day 45

It's not about always having a man; it's about having the right man.

Consider that you have a man but he doesn't appreciate you, doesn't show you love, shouts at rather that speaks to you, cheats on you, tells lies, is unambitious and takes you for granted – sure, you have a man, but is he the right man for you? Is he the type of man you want? Having a man does not and should not give you bragging rights, particularly if you have the sort of man described here. Certain women make a big deal about letting other women (single) know about their man. Who needs a man if he does not love you, appreciate you and treat you right? It's really not about having a man; it's about having the right man who will treat you right.

Day 46

Sometimes you have to let people go because the stress they bring into your life isn't worth it.

Day 47

Accepting responsibility, saying I'm sorry and asking for forgiveness are not signs of weakness in a relationship – they are signs of strength.

Day 48

Happiness - is what passes you by as you wait for him to change.

Day 49

Trust - easy to break, hard to rebuild.

Day 50

I don't want an on and off relationship. I want a relationship that's always on.

Many people fall into this very unhealthy cycle of on and off relationships. And what happens during the off cycles can be shocking as some men use it as an excuse to see other women. Do you really want an on and off relationship? I didn't think so. You should look for a relationship that is always 'on.' Naturally, your relationship will have disagreements and at times be faced with challenges, which you can both resolve together in a civil manner, or at least try to. Constant disagreements or issues that leads to constant breaking up is unhealthy. Breaking up to make up becomes emotionally draining after a while.

Day 51

A man must come up to your level. Don't stoop to his.

Day 52

The best relationships are formed from the fact that it's not so much that you love him but that he also loves you.

Day 53

After a failed relationship, do not wrap yourself in the arms of another - wrap yourself in you.

Day 54

While we want to believe what we are told, for your heart's sake believe what you are shown.

Day 55

A woman who knows what she wants is not picky; she just knows what she wants.

It's a common fallacy amongst some men that if a woman isn't into him, tells him where he falls short in her expectations or simply tells him what she wants, then such a woman is picky or even a bitch. It's the modern day equivalent of that age old saying, "When the fox can't get the grapes………" Some men seem to have a great deal of difficulty understanding women. It could be that they group all women together, don't take the time to understand women or are too deeply entrenched in a stereotypical world that equates women who speak up and say what they want with being picky. In your list of expectations for men you should have an entry for a man who either understands you or is willing to take the time to do so.

Day 56

Time is precious; not everyone is worthy of your time.

Day 57

If your heart isn't in it, you shouldn't stay in it.

Day 58

You should not be with a man only because you love him but because he also loves you.

Day 59

Women are priceless but can cheapen themselves by the way they allow men to treat them.

Day 60

If he wants you, you won't have to chase him.

Pretty simple quote requiring little explanation. The man who wants you won't require you to chase after him. By chasing, I'm not referring to subtle hints you give that he may or may not get. I'm referring to you actively pursuing him: buying gifts, constant phone calls and text messages, asking him out on numerous occasions, hanging out at his favorite spots, hoping he sees you, etc... When a man wants you he lets you know by his actions. If you are chasing him chances are he's too busy chasing someone else, not you.

Day 61

Men change only if they want to. Wanting or trying to change him is a
waste of your time – invest that time in you.

Day 62

Strong confident women do not lower their morals and standards to be in a
relationship – they expect their expectations to be met and view
compromise as necessary for a relationship to work.

Day 63

It's not about being loyal to a man; it's about being loyal to your heart.

Day 64

Love does not come in the night and leave in the morning.

Day 65

When the relationship becomes exhausting, it is time to give it a rest – permanently.

Being in a relationship should not be a tiring undertaking. When you are away from him you shouldn't dread going home to him or meeting him. When he calls you, your attitude should not be, "Oh, it's you." With all of life's challenges, your relationship should be one that you enjoy and is stress free. It should put a smile on your face not a frown. If the events or lack thereof in your relationship seems to be dragging you down and making you emotionally weary, then it's time to give that relationship a rest.

Day 66

Make sure you are in love and not in love with hope – the man you hoped he would be.

Day 67

Don't confuse lust with love; lust is immediate, love grows.

Day 68

You don't have to tell a real man how to treat you.

Day 69

When a man tells you, you'd never find another like him, he's right - you'll find better.

Day 70

Sometimes you have to choose you over him.

Maybe he's a great catch. Maybe he's the best thing you've ever had and you find yourself going crazy over him. Perhaps, you've not yet had him and you are hoping, wanting and trying to make him yours. In all of your antics to get him or keep him, you should ask yourself, "What is he doing to keep/get me?" Your desire to have or to keep a man should not continue to the point where you are losing yourself in obsessing over him. Sometimes you are the only one working to keep the relationship alive. Is he really worth you changing and becoming someone one else? Sometimes you have to choose yourself over a man for your emotional well-being, your sanity, and to give yourself the opportunity to meet a well-intentioned man who will choose you.

Day 71

If there is no honesty and trust, there is no relationship, just two people sleeping with each other.

Day 72

Real men do not disrespect women – not even accidentally.

Day 73

His words might grab your attention but let his actions grab your heart.

Day 74

Having a "friend" on the side in case your relationship does not work out is proof that you are not ready for a committed relationship.

Day 75

Do not be afraid of starting over; sometimes it is exactly what you need.

You are miserable in your relationship, complaining, unhappy, feeling unloved and unappreciated. You know that the solution to your problem is to leave but you are afraid to do so. You think it's a daunting task having to start all over again and meeting someone new. You rationalize that even though you aren't happy in your current relationship at least you "know" him. Even if you "know" him, apparently you don't know him well enough to be happy with him. You can be complacent, trying to find what good thing about the miserable relationship you can hold onto to, in order to justify staying. The truth is that sometimes you simply need to get out, move on and start over because it's where your happiness awaits.

Day 76

Strong independent women know they are not defined by men – they define themselves.

Day 77

Some things in your relationship should not be given the opportunity to happen again – once is enough.

Day 78

You can only make so many attempts to mend a broken relationship because at some point those continued attempts begin to break you.

Day 79

As your biological clock winds down, make sure your standards for men don't wind down as well.

Day 80

Don't let him have you while he decides if he wants you.

Hmmm, ladies, let's think about this. I'm not sure if I want to be with you or have a relationship with you. However, while I decide, if I ever do, let us continue to have sex. Does that sound familiar to you? It's possible that at some point, you and your man were both feeling things out in terms of how serious you should become. You, months or years ago, decided that you'd like to be serious but he hasn't. You are still waiting! At some point, you have to know definitively what he wants to do. Don't allow him to have you as an extended booty call – has sex with you but you have no relationship status with him. Your status to him reads as, "Deciding if I want to be with her." With such a status he may never commit to you because while he is still "deciding" you allow him to continue sleeping with you.

Day 81

Some of the best relationships are the ones you never saw coming.

Day 82

Looking for a man is not the same as looking for love – men are easy to find.

Day 83

You are perfect for the man who loves and accepts you with all your imperfections.

Day 84

A relationship is an investment – you invest your time, love and emotions. Like all investments, it should be thoroughly checked out before you invest.

Day 85

A beautiful relationship is worth waiting for.

There is never a need to rush into a relationship despite ticking biological clocks, nagging parents, peer pressure from girlfriends and anxious overzealous men wanting to marry you tomorrow! Beautiful relationships develop over time and are well worth the wait – waiting for the right man for you.

Day 86

Sometimes you know exactly who you want to spend your life with – if only they felt the same.

Day 87

Afraid of the single life, a woman can jump from one relationship to the next, never finding or knowing what she wants...and she will not until she develops the most important relationship – the one with herself.

Day 88

Your happiness depends on you, not him... you have to do what's necessary to make you happy.

Day 89

A failed relationship does not mean you lost everything. Sometimes that failed relationship is everything you need to move on.

Day 90

When you realize he is the wrong man, staying won't make him become the right one.

Oops, you made a mistake! It happens in life more times than we would like. However, when you realize a relationship mistake such as being in it with the wrong person, you need to get out – fast. Staying won't make him become the right one. If he's not the one, he's not the one. You need to get out, move on, and find the one for you.

Day 91

Frustrated, some women lower their expectations for a man without realizing they are lowering themselves.

Day 92

Hearts are delicate, fragile, and only to be entrusted to the one who has demonstrated that he can and will take care of it – your heart is no different.

Day 93

Don't get a man because all your friends have; get a man because he is deserving of you.

Day 94

If you are not valued, respected, and appreciated then you are in the wrong relationship.

Day 95

A man might take away your belief in love, trust, and relationships, but never let him take away your belief in you and what you can do.

It is possible that because you so loved and trusted this man his actions severely shook your belief in love and trust. There are times when the actions of another person was something you never envisioned, never saw coming because it was a direct contradiction to who that person was or portrayed himself to be. When someone acts in a matter that shakes the very foundation of your belief system, don't let it shake your belief in you. You are resilient, you are strong, and even though you will at times fall and fail, you will rise from that fall and you will eventually succeed. No man, via actions or words, can take away the spirit of you. You should not let him because you are stronger than he is you just haven't dug deep enough within you.

Day 96

Love - its actions, not words.

Day 97

You don't ask him to set you free; you free yourself from him.

Day 98

If he does not want you as much as you want him its best that you both move on – particularly you.

Day 99

Appreciate the man who was considerate enough to reveal his baggage – he gave you a choice.

Day 100

Strong independent women intimidate weak men.

Maybe it's their mindset – women should be domesticated, docile and submissive – or maybe they themselves are simply threatened by or cannot deal with an independent woman. Men who are intimidated (which can take many forms) by strong independent women are usually weak-minded, not on your level and don't warrant your time. Seek a man who embraces, applauds and encourages your independence. Avoid men who hide behind a "masculine" world.

Day 101

When the relationship gets to the point where he is there but not there and you are always there, it's time for you to be elsewhere.

Day 102

Some relationships ended before they even began; you just ignored the signs or you thought he'd change.

Day 103

At times the biggest obstacle to your happiness is the person in the mirror.

Day 104

Being with a man is not the same as being in a relationship with him.

Day 105

Find someone to love you for who you are and not what he wants you to be; if he can't love you for you then he is not the one.

Our desire to love is strong and sometimes that desire can change who we are in terms of our behavior and sometimes beliefs. Love should never be about changing your core beliefs, principles and morals. That love requires compromise is a true statement; however, sometimes a man wants you to change who you are as a person because that's the way he wants you to be. The belief is that if he can mold you or shape you into what he wants then he would be happy with you. Hold on!!! Do you see the selfishness of that mindset? If he wants to change or mold you a particular why is he even with you? There are men out there who would love you just the way you are and you won't have to change a thing about you.

Day 106

Do not assume you are in a relationship unless you both agree.

Day 107

Love is patient, loneliness is not – do not be a victim of the impatience of loneliness.

Day 108

If in your relationship you are smiling on the outside but dying on the inside, get into one where you are smiling both inside and outside.

Day 109

You don't raise your self-esteem by lowering your standards.

Day 110

If you are a good woman, he should see that. You cannot make him see something he can't or won't, and if he doesn't then perhaps he is not the one.

A self-explanatory quote to the core. You don't have to tell and you should not have to remind a man about your caring and loving nature. That you are there for him or have been there for him through the rough and the good times should be obvious. You don't have to give a man a resume of your qualities. The right man will be with you because he sees what a good woman you are and that was what attracted him to you. If you are currently trying to convince your man to see what a good woman you are then perhaps he's not your man; he was meant to be with someone else.

Day 111

Not all men are relationship material and it's best to realize this sooner rather than later.

Day 112

Little things that are big – a text message, a call, a hug, a smile, a touch...

Day 113

It's better to be single than to be miserable, lonely, and unhappy in a relationship.

Day 114

The person who loves you will prioritize you accordingly. Don't worry about where you are on their list; prioritize you and what's important to you.

Day 115

The men who tell you that your standards and expectations are too high are the men who know they have fallen short.

If he confidently measures up to your expectations, it's highly doubtful that you'd hear such rhetoric. Keeping your high standards and expectations for men is a sure fire way of keeping out the men in whom you have no interest. High standards and expectations simply means you are not interested in lying, cheating, deadbeat men. It means you are looking for a man who will appreciate and respect you and knows how to treat and love you. It means you expect him to have particular characteristics, personality, principles and morals. High expectations and standards does not mean—well, it should not mean—you are looking for millionaires, because there are many millionaires who believe that their money, wealth and influence can get them everything, including you and others. Your high standards and expectations should not have a monetary price tag.

Day 116

Men who do not know and appreciate your worth are not worth your time.

Day 117

When you settle for less knowing you deserve more you have marked your value down.

Day 118

In a relationship, maturity is measured by actions.

Day 119

Differences: Most men want the woman but not the relationship; most women want the man and the relationship.

Day 120

If you are the only one who cares about the relationship maybe it's time to find someone who cares about you.

A relationship is about two individuals who want to be together and are together enjoying each other, shared moments, special moments and moving forward together in life. Hence, obviously, if you are the only one who cares about the relationship or wants the relationship, there is a problem. Why should you be the one putting forth time and energy to make it work if the other person has demonstrated that they don't care? Instead of being on an emotional treadmill, going nowhere fast, it's better to get off and seek someone who wants to be in a relationship with you.

Day 121

Some men are like leaky rooftops—they look good in the summer but you won't know they leak unless you see what happens when it rains. It takes time to get to know a man.

Day 122

I love you – the three most frequently-abused words, frequently said without understanding their meaning, used to pacify, used as a means to an end and often confused with sexual desire or infatuation – men should say this only when they mean it and can show it.

Day 123

While it is not mandatory to have a man, if you are looking, it is mandatory that you know what you are looking for in him.

Day 124

Promises: Sometimes another word for lies.

Day 125

Sometimes the best way is to go separate ways.

Dragging out a relationship in which you are unhappy or he is unhappy is emotional torture. As adults, you should know when it is time to move on. The sense of knowing when to move on should happen particularly after either you or both of you have tried to make it work— with little success—or he has repeatedly broken your heart. Staying in such a relationship prevents you from engaging in another relationship that might be the true relationship for you. Yes, leaving can be tough, hard, and difficult, but staying can be frustrating, unhappy and downright depressing. My guess is you'd like to be in a happy relationship.

Day 126

Loneliness can lead to temptation and with temptation things sometimes appear better than they really are.

Day 127

You can't love someone if you don't trust him because love implies trust.

Day 128

Personality makes the man.

Day 129

Short-term pleasures may become long-term pain – make wise decisions.

Day 130

It's human to make mistakes; it's foolish not to learn from them.

As it pertains to relationships, one should try to get it right the first time. Though there are no guarantees, there are things one can do to increase the possibility of having a long and loving relationship. Know what you want, take your time, set high expectations for you and him, be willing to compromise without losing yourself, etc... As humans, it is inevitable that mistakes will be made; however, it is your responsibility to learn from them. Don't cry—well, not too long—over mistakes made. Rather, it behooves you to reflect and see what, how or where it went wrong. The next step is to take those lessons learned and apply them toward your next relationship.

Day 131

They are called self-esteem, self-confidence, and self-worth for a reason –
they do not depend on him.

Day 132

Don't let your fear of losing him make you lose who you are.

Day 133

Seek love...it outlives lust and infatuation.

Day 134

Do not have a child because you think it is going to make him remain with
you – he will not; only his resentment of you will remain.

Day 135

Be careful that in "holding on" to him you're not letting go of you. It's not a matter of doing whatever you can to hold on to him. If you view your relationship as one in which you have to do "whatever" you can to hold on to him, hopefully he's doing whatever he can to also hold on to you.

Sometimes, the fear of losing a man can subconsciously let you lose yourself as you make desperate attempts to keep him. You may even try to become a different person because you think he wants you to be different. If you compromise your age-old principles and beliefs, then you no longer are the person you were. Why do all this for a man who shouldn't put you in such a position to begin with?

Day 136

A vulnerability we face as humans is our desire to have someone; however, we must be careful that our vulnerability does not rule our actions lest we become more vulnerable.

Day 137

Sometimes, someone is not "your type" until you get to know them and vice versa, someone is "your type" until you get to know them – it takes time to know someone.

Day 138

Understand that while you may want a man, having one does not guarantee all the emotional things you need.

Day 139

If your fear is losing your man to another woman, either he is not the right one or you are more insecure than you thought – a woman cannot "steal" your man.

$\mathcal{D}ay$ 140

You have to be happy with yourself before you can be happy with someone else.

Think about it—would you want to be in a relationship with a miserable man? The reverse is true; no man wants to be in a relationship with you if you are miserable and dealing with your unresolved issues. The fact of the matter is that we should try to be in that inward happy place before looking outward to get into a relationship. Getting into a relationship begins with you. You have to be happy, wanting and ready to be in a relationship. Love yourself and be happy with you before asking someone to love and be happy with you.

Day 141

Single – willing to wait for what you want.

Day 142

You can only do so much to keep him and hold onto the relationship;
sometimes you just have to let go.

Day 143

True beauty lies in our character, which is revealed over time, and cannot
be masked by looks. Sadly, some overlook the inner beauty or lack thereof
in someone because they focus on how the person looks.

Day 144

Love doesn't exist only in the bedroom.

Day 145

Sometimes you get cheated on twice; he cheated on you and you cheated yourself by being with him.

This quote arises from the sad situation of you possibly ignoring the red flags, advice of your friends and your own intuition and plunging into a relationship with him. Then you discover that he's the opposite of what was initially portrayed. The charade was dropped and the real person that he is was finally revealed and... you didn't like it. Upon this discovery, the remorseful, regretful emotions surface as you finally realize that you should not have been with him in the first place. You could have avoided your current troubles.

Day 146

There is nothing wrong with rushing into the arms of a man as long as you take time to know him before you get there.

Day 147

Sometimes it's more fun just knowing someone rather than being in a relationship with him – not everyone you get along with is relationship material.

Day 148

Relationship building is done by two people. If one person isn't, then you're not building a relationship.

Day 149

Single – it makes you appreciate you.

Day 150

What's important to you may not necessarily be important to him, but a good man supports you either way.

Here is a perfect example of why you should not have a man just for the sake of saying or telling others you have one. I've repeatedly stated in this book that a man physically being with you is not the same as a man who is both physically and emotionally there with/for you. If you are involved in something that's important to you, then, your good man, though he may not necessarily be interested in whatever you are involved with, will still support you because he loves you. If it's important to you, it becomes important to him.

Day 151

If your heart keeps getting broken maybe it opens up too easily.

Day 152

Your failure to let go of the hurt of past relationships can prevent you from having future relationships.

Day 153

While his words may hurt you, they should never break you.

Day 154

When you stop accepting less, you open yourself to receiving more – the more that you deserve.

Day 155

Any relationship in which you are free to be yourself without judgment from your significant other is a wonderful relationship.

A relationship should not change you at your core in a negative manner. Certainly, you can have a man who inspired you to perhaps discover your true potential or stop some destructive behaviors like smoking or gambling, etc... A man telling you that you laugh too much or too loudly, that you are too caring, or a man who wants you to change your principles and core beliefs is not allowing you to be yourself. In such a situation, you are being stifled and feel you have to always be guarded around him. Be with someone who is comfortable and accepts who you are as a person. Always be with someone who allows you to be you and you don't feel like you have to walk on egg shells around him.

Day 156

If he wants or expects sex on the first date then perhaps he should not expect a second date.

Day 157

You can only give so much of yourself; you have to know when you've given enough.

Day 158

Sometimes you have to cut a relationship short to stand a better chance of getting into a long one.

Day 159

You don't have to "sell" yourself to a man because the man who wants you will "buy" you just the way you are.

Day 160

Every woman is a precious diamond but not every man is a "jeweler" that knows how to keep, care, appreciate and treasure her – find yourself a good jeweler.

Yes, you are! Even though some of you may be diamonds in the rough, a diamond is a diamond. There is a particular way you should be treated. You don't want to be in a relationship where you are not valued, disrespected, taken for granted or ignored. You want to be happy and secure, free to express yourself and be yourself. Unfortunately, not every man knows how to cultivate the relationship to allow these wonderful things to happen. You are precious and you should be treated preciously. Find a man that values, treasures and treats you accordingly. You deserve it.

Day 161

Be impressed with what he says but fall for what he does.

Day 162

The real blueprint for finding a man is yours - your expectations, what you accept or allow, and the amount of time you give yourself to know him.

Day 163

Whether he's a liar, abuser, unappreciative or selfish, the choice to stay is yours – difficult at times but still your choice.

Day 164

When a man understands you, he ceases to be judgmental because he listens to all that you have to say because he invested time in knowing you.

Day 165

Men are simple; they treat you the way you allow them to treat you.

If you allow a man to ill-treat, disrespect, lie and cheat on you, he is most likely going to continue to do so. Hence it is important that you let a man understand what your expectations are. Whenever he falls short in one or more of those areas, it is your responsibility to let him know or you should take action that sends him a message.

Day 166

It's not that you haven't had a man in a long time, it's about waiting a long time to find the right man.

Day 167

Your relationship should be built on the reciprocity of love, trust, respect and appreciation.

Day 168

How indecisive is he, if he can't decide to be in a relationship with you but he has decided to sleep with you in the interim?

Day 169

There are few things money can't buy – one of them should be you.

Day 170

You can't share a broken you; you have to make yourself whole before you can share yourself again.

It takes time to heal. The healing process is not a rushed one and should not be tied to a particular timeframe. If you are broken from a bad relationship you should take the time necessary for you to feel mended and be whole once more. It's unfair of you, though you can for selfish reasons, to try and share yourself with someone while you are still broken. It's also grossly unfair to the other person, if they can't have the mended you. Would you like a still emotionally wounded and broken man to be with you?

Day 171

Get a man that "gets" you.

Day 172

A man should never "look" like the one; he should act it.

Day 173

A man who fails to appreciate his woman will himself not be appreciated.

Day 174

If you want to make him yours, it works better if he wants to make you his.

Day 175

It's not easy closing your heart to someone to whom it was always open but sometimes they leave you with no other choice.

Amazing how that once powerful feeling of being in love with someone can fade. And because love is such a powerful emotion, it can make things difficult or it can do the opposite. If you've been hurt, depending on your feelings, you may want to leave. However, sometimes the emotional hurt that was inflicted leaves you no choice but to leave because staying is more painful.

Day 176

If a man keeps coming in and out of your life it's only because you let him.

Day 177

Quickly getting into another relationship is not the way to get over a failed one.

Day 178

One of the easiest ways to gain respect is to first respect yourself.

Day 179

Games do not belong in a relationship. If he's into playing games best to let him play by or with himself.

Day 180

Sometimes, your perfect relationship package does not come wrapped tall, dark and handsome.

Your expectations for a man should be more about his character, personality, principles and morals and less about his physique. I absolutely understand that in almost all cases you won't seek a relationship with someone who does not fit your physical profile. Yet, sometimes, women end up with someone whose looks and physique were not what they were originally attracted to. If he has all of the characteristics, personality, principles and morals you envisioned but he's not tall, dark and handsome, do you ignore him? Some of the best relationships were formed when least expected and with the least expected individual...be open.

Day 181

If relationships take work, it's definitely not a one-person job.

Day 182

Single is not a death sentence; it's a life experience from which you gain strength and independence.

Day 183

Fiercely guard your heart but when you surrender do so willing and without reservations.

Day 184

Moving on does not mean forgetting all that happened; it means taking the lessons learned and applying them toward a better relationship in the future.

Day 185

Don't look for a man to complete you, complete yourself first then look for a man.

There is much to do and accomplish before you start looking for a man. One of the things I urge you to do before getting into a relationship is to seek to become independent both financially and mentally. To be independent financially is to be in a job, have a business or be on a career path that reaps or will reap you financial rewards such that you don't need support from a man (although this gets more complicated with children). Also, you should mentally develop yourself to be an independent thinker capable of having your own ideas and making your own decisions. Develop a sense of self-awareness, get to know yourself, your likes and dislikes and your comfort zone. It has to be all about you before you make it all about you and a man. Before him, there was you and you will always be relevant.

Day 186

Your worth is not defined by what others think of you; it's in your own perception and belief of self and how you project that onto others.

Day 187

It's not about the quantity of men who want your number; it's the quality.

Day 188

Great relationships are built on trust; trust must be earned and earning takes time.

Day 189

The more time you spend being bitter the less time you have for happiness.

Day 190

Men chase but only you decide who'll catch you.

It's the basic instinct of men – to pursue a woman. However, it doesn't mean that of the multitude of men that come on to you all are worthy of you. Always remember that you are in control of what happens in your interactions with men. A man chasing you is doing what men do; you, being careful, selective, diligent and guarded are doing what you ought to do. It's your choice which man "catches" you.

Day 191

Compatibility is not determined by looks.

Day 192

It's not fair to you when you stay with someone whom you know is not the one – you deserve better and he doesn't deserve you.

Day 193

The best first impression you will ever make on a man – be yourself.

Day 194

Men don't get stolen; they leave.

Day 195

If you remain in an unhealthy or unhappy relationship to avoid being lonely, you already are.

Many times in life we doubt ourselves. We doubt what we can do. The truth is that in many of these doubtful circumstances, we can do all of those things we somehow think we can't. At times we know what we have to do but we don't do it because the task seems daunting. It's really not. Leaving a relationship is always an option, but it's an option that many of us don't exercise as frequently as we should. If you are afraid to leave an unhappy or an unhealthy relationship because you fear being lonely, then you are operating under a false sense of security. The truth is, under such circumstances, you are emotionally alone. Being with someone because they are physically there is not the same as having an emotionally supportive person or environment. People in healthy, emotionally stable relationships don't typically want to leave. You don't have to be alone to be lonely. If your emotional needs and desires aren't being met or fully satisfied in your relationship you are lonely.

Day 196

Don't look for love where it isn't.

Day 197

After you've discovered the lies, it's difficult to see past them and find truth in anything else he says.

Day 198

Unhealthy relationship – the more you give the more they take but the more you ask for the less they give.

Day 199

Your self-esteem is like a fence; if it is low then anyone can climb over it.

Day 200

It's his choice to have multiple women but your choice not to be one of them.

Complaining about his multiple women will not necessarily stop him from having them. Making the choice to leave means he can keep his multiple women but you won't be one of them. And why should you stay? You deserve someone who is dedicated and committed to you. Someone who can and should focus his attention only on you, not share it with other women.

Day 201

That I am single does not mean I am lonely.

Day 202

Dating in desperation is like drowning –you grab at anything.

Day 203

It's an unfair fight if you are the only one fighting to keep the relationship.

Day 204

A strong solid relationship transcends the physical and is built on other elements such as love, mutual respect, appreciation, emotional support, friendship, compromise, and understanding.

Day 205

Do not confuse men with items in a store; what you see isn't always what you get.

Being with a man or selecting him based upon how he looks would only work if you could also simultaneously see his character, personality, morals and principles. Unfortunately, what you see is not always what you get when it comes to men. You have to "look" longer and by that I mean get to know him before you decide to "buy" him.

Day 206

When we stop communicating the relationship starts dying.

Day 207

A relationship is between two people but when a third person enters into it, it's an indication that someone has gotten selfish.

Day 208

The little things you keep sweeping under the carpet will eventually grow into something you can no longer hide - always communicate.

Day 209

A failed relationship does not mean you are a failure, it means that particular relationship was not for you.

Day 210

Don't try to mold a man into what you want him to be; if you're with him it's because you accept him for whom or what he is.

Unless you're in the pottery business, stop trying to mold a man or change him into your likeness. The last time you checked, you were not God, creating someone in your own image and likeness. Men change only if they want to change. Granted, you can try to influence him, coach and coax him but it's futile if he does not want to change. Then you should ask yourself: why try to mold a man when you can go out and find one that requires no molding?

Day 211

I can't think of a good reason to rush into a relationship, can you?

Day 212

If he has moved on, so should you. You can't hold on to someone who has already left.

Day 213

The only thing you should take with you from a bad relationship is the lesson learned – not the man.

Day 214

Relationships are easier to maintain when both people want it.

Day 215

Conversations reveal a lot about someone. Take the time to have conversations – they can either start or rightfully prevent a relationship from happening.

Choosing to move or jump right into a relationship simply based upon the person's looks or a couple of selected words you hear from them is asinine. Sure, you might be physically attracted to him, but if you are looking for a serious relationship, not just sex, then your next step is to engage him in conversations. You'd be surprised at how many men look good but once you start having a real conversation with them you realize that their looks and physique are all that they have. Some men look good and that's it! They can't hold your interest with good intelligent conversations. At times, you might make the bonus discovery that, in addition to looking good, he can also have meaningful conversations that will hold your interest and mentally stimulate you.

Day 216

Married but lonely, in a relationship yet single, happy on the outside but sad on the inside, unfulfilled desires and dreams – such is the life of the woman who has settled or sold herself short.

Day 217

Self-esteem, self-confidence, and self-worth comes from "self" – you have to believe in you.

Day 218

If you're the only one defending his behavior, maybe it's time to take a second look at what you're defending.

Day 219

While everyone can change, not everyone wants to change. It's best you realize this sooner rather than later. Stop trying to change him.

Day 220

"I love you" does not mean I am an endless source of forgiveness.

Lets' face it, men and women are different. This difference is magnified when we look at our emotional behaviors and expectations. Some men play upon that emotional difference very well. You love to hear the words, "I love you," particularly if you believe the person. Sadly, men know this and so some of us use that as an excuse when we hurt you. You should not fall for a man repeatedly hurting you and using the "I love you" excuse to get your forgiveness. When a man loves you, he does not hurt you. A man constantly asking you for forgiveness is contradicting his professed love for you by his opposite actions.

Day 221

Sometimes the grass is only greener on the other side until you get there.

Day 222

An appreciative man is grateful, recognizes and acknowledges his woman's full worth and contributions to the relationship. His appreciation is demonstrated.

Day 223

One way to find out if you are in a true relationship is to strip away the physical and see what's left.

Day 224

A black eye and busted lips do not come from the hands of someone who loves you.

Day 225

A relationship is a two-way street but some people clog both lanes with their selfishness and inconsiderate behaviors.

A relationship should be the union or the coming together of two individuals who want to be with each other. And within that relationship, each individual should reciprocate love, caring, compromise, unselfishness and appreciation for the other person. Unfortunately, some individuals didn't get the memo, don't seem to understand what's involved in a relationship, or never wanted to be in a relationship. Whatever the reason(s), they act selfishly and engage in behaviors that are hurtful to the relationship.

Day 226

Compromise is a necessary ingredient for a relationship to work.

Day 227

The unspoken word is as important as the spoken word. In a relationship, you "listen" to the unspoken word by looking at actions.

Day 228

Sometimes you can't and shouldn't go back.

Day 229

Good men are hard to find because there are too many imposters in the way.

Day 230

Because the relationship fell apart, you don't have to fall apart.

It's tough to have a relationship end, particularly one in which you loved the person and you didn't want it to be over. It can be emotionally stressful as you go through and deal with the accompanying range of emotions. It's natural and it's okay to cry. It's normal that for a couple of days immediately following the end of the relationship you might perhaps not want to eat, socialize, answer your phone, etc. Maybe you have difficulty sleeping. However, months later, you should not be feeling as if the breakup just happened. Face the reality, slowly look forward and don't get stuck in the past, he moved on without you and you must without him.

Day 231

Sometimes letting go is better than holding on.

Day 232

Life gets busy sometimes and unexpected things happen. However, we should still find a little time for the ones we love to let them know that despite being busy they are in our thoughts – and they should do likewise.

Day 233

What he does and what you accept helps define your relationship.

Day 224

Blaming someone else without acknowledging your own fault(s) is a selfish trait; many relationships have ended because of selfishness.

Day 225

The people who can't accept you for who you are, are the people not meant to be with you.

You should not have to force, beg, plead or use subtle tactics to get someone to stay with you because they don't accept you the way you are. By the same token, you should not have to change so that they can accept you. You are who you are, they are who they are. Sometimes, compromise does not bridge the differences. Be mindful of the fact that there is someone out there for you that requires absolutely no change in you. Likewise, there's someone out there for him whom he can accept just the way that person is. Let's not make it too complicated, he either is or isn't for you.

Day 226

Bad relationships are everywhere. Suffering in one is optional.

Day 227

Self – one of the most important relationships you can have. If you can't have a good relationship with yourself it's difficult for others to have one with you.

Day 228

Sometimes it's best to say goodbye before saying hello.

Day 229

When you view relationships through desperation and ticking clocks, you see things you want to see instead of what's actually there.

Day 230

While men may be in abundance, "relationship material" men are few – choose wisely.

Not all men are relationship material. Most men want you but not a relationship with you. The challenge is for you to focus on the men who are relationship material. How do you do that? Well, since most men will tell you they are relationship material because it's easy to say so, the next step is for you to let them, over time, show it. It's all in a man's actions.

Day 231

It's the simple things that builds great relationships.

Day 232

A woman clothed in humility, unselfishness, compromise and love is just as sexy and appealing to the man who can see beyond the superficial.

Day 233

Relationships entered into for the wrong reasons usually go wrong.

Day 234

Arguments or disagreements with your significant other should not be about who wins. If there's a winner it means there is a loser and in a healthy and happy relationship there should be no losers, just two winners – you and him.

$\mathcal{D}ay$ 235

A man can only continue to ill-treat, disrespect and fail to appreciate you if you continue to stay.

You, despite what you think of yourself, deserve to be happy in your relationship. If you are in an unhappy relationship where you are ill-treated, taken for granted, not loved and not appreciated, then you need to get out of it. At times it is difficult to leave because of children, assets, lack of independence and the embarrassment of what family and friends might say. However, if after repeatedly trying to make him change his treatment of and attitude towards you, you have no luck, then you must seriously consider the choice of leaving. If you stay, he will, most likely, continue his ill treatment of you. By staying in such a relationship he won't see a reason to change his treatment of you.

Day 236

There is a lot you can do and achieve without a man – you simply haven't tried hard enough.

Day 237

If he quickly gets to "I love you" it doesn't mean that you have to quickly get there too.

Day 238

Moments of weakness are a test of your strength.

Day 239

If you feel chained and locked in your relationship don't forget you have the key.

Day 240

Make sure you know him before you start talking about "us" and "we."

I've heard men talked about feeling rushed after going on just a couple of dates with women. Or sometimes they detect desperation in what the women have said. If the first date went well, it's not the start of a relationship; it's an indication there's a strong possibility of a second date. A first date is also not an appropriate occasion to launch into discussions involving a future of "us" and "we." Such discussions are a turn off for men and a huge red flag. You have to know a man and you should take the time to know him before you start speaking in such a manner. And even if you believe you know him well enough, tread carefully... make sure he also wants the same. While men may rush you into bed, they don't like being rushed into a relationship.

Day 241

A second chance should not be automatic, it should be earned.

Day 242

I know you don't love me because your actions says so.

Day 243

Don't spend a lifetime regretting that which cannot be undone; it's best to view regret as a learning experience.

Day 244

I don't care that everyone lies. I don't want you lying to me.

Day 245

One of his responsibilities is to provide you the security of knowing that you shouldn't have insecurities.

In a relationship you want to have the comfort of being secure. Secure in his love, secure that he wants the relationship as much as you do and secure in his commitment to you. Insecurities, if warranted, based upon his actions or lack thereof can stifle and suffocate your relationship. It can be emotionally draining to constantly wonder about trust issues and the longevity of your relationship. Your man, by his actions, should make you feel secure rather than insecure.

Day 246

Stop searching for the good in him; the good should be obvious.

Day 247

We all have baggage, some heavier than others; the problem occurs when you are not told about his baggage or just how heavy it is.

Day 248

The men you attract are not always a reflection of you – only the ones you choose.

Day 249

Relationship appreciation is an acknowledgment, verbal or non-verbal, of your presence, your value, your contribution and your dedication to him. Are you appreciated?

Day 250

The best way to keep a relationship is to have one worth keeping.

I frequently muse on how quickly middle school boys and girls say that they are dating someone new. I once taught middle school and it seemed as if the girls dated a new boy every week. You are long past that age and if you are changing relationships from week to week, or month to month, it is an indication of a possible problem – bad choices made, expectations or lack thereof, low self-esteem, etc... If you want a long-lasting and fulfilling relationship then look for one that is worth keeping. While no guarantees are given, you can certainly enhance the possibility of a worthy relationship by: having your list of expectations, taking time to know him, ensuring he wants the same for the relationship and that you both are committed to making it work. See, it's not always about getting in, it's about staying in the relationship.

Day 251

Your dignity, value, and self-worth are much more important than your need for the security of having a man – never ever compromise those.

Day 252

You are capable of and deserve much more, but you limit yourself by thinking you can't or by settling – many times you are your own obstacle.

Day 253

Don't choose someone based on how you feel about yourself, but rather on how you both feel about each other.

Day 254

More important than the relationship you lost is the experience you gained.

Day 255

Learn to avoid the avoidable in relationships: be patient, listen don't just hear, look past looks, be logical, and definitely don't sell yourself short.

Once again there are no guarantees about how long your relationship might last but there are certain things you can do to increase the likelihood of being in a long-lasting relationship. Patience in waiting for the right man can possibly lead to your expectations being met. Listen to what he says. Listening is an art and is not the same as hearing. Focus on his character, personalities, morals and values. Be logical; he must make sense in what he says and does. Don't be mesmerized by looks or impressive word choices. Look for substance and don't be swayed by superficial things about a man.

Day 256

Don't be too hard on you. If you've done and given your all and you're still unhappy you can move on without guilt – and you should.

Day 257

There is no shortage of men, just good men.

Day 258

An understanding man —one who knows that sometimes it's only about cuddling, respects your boundaries, lets you be you and doesn't make you feel pressured.

Day 259

It's okay if a man leaves you; it's not okay if men are always leaving you.

Day 260

The best protector of your heart is you.

If hearts are broken by whom you let in, then it is your responsibility to ensure that he is worthy of being let into your heart. Men who you want to let into your heart should be screened using your list of expectations. Although screening might sometimes fail (he lied, you rushed, etc...) it's better than not screening at all. Protect your heart by making smart choices in men.

Day 261

If you keep forgiving, he'll keep seeking forgiveness – at some point enough is enough.

Day 262

True character lies beneath physical appearance – always look for true character.

Day 263

Real women know a man's hurtful words do not define her; she defines herself.

Day 264

Try loving yourself first – it makes a difference.

Day 265

When we rush, we make mistakes; this is also true of relationships.

Ever had to rush to leave the house only to realize you left something or you didn't satisfactorily accessorize yourself? Well, when you rush into a relationship you also make mistakes, big ones. You might forget to look for certain things and you also might overlook things. Unlike leaving the house in a rush and forgetting your eye shadow, lipstick or your matching bracelet, the emotional toll can be huge with relationship mistakes. You can't undo sleeping with a man whom you quickly realized was not the man for you. You can't undo the fact that you were caught up in his words and his looks so you didn't look further or take the time to see that he was an arrogant self-righteous idiot. It didn't work out because you didn't take time to know him past his looks, words, appearance, clothes, etc... A tough lesson but hopefully you'll take those lessons into the next relationship.

Day 266

Women want to believe men, but most men believe they should lie to women and therein lies the problem.

Day 267

It takes time to know you; give your time to the one willing to give you his time.

Day 268

Not all relationships were meant to end in a marriage; sometimes it's still successful because of what you learned and discovered about yourselves.

Day 269

In your haste to find Mr. Right, you may end up with Mr. Wrong.

Day 270

If he can't respect you, he can't be with you.

While compromise is a necessary ingredient to make a relationship work, it does not mean that you'll compromise on everything. Some things can't or shouldn't be up for compromise. That he must respect you at all times is not up for compromise. If he can't respect you, he shouldn't be with you.

Day 271

A man should make you feel special in your relationship because you are. If you don't feel special in your relationship with him, then, maybe, he's not the special man for you.

Day 272

A man who is paying your bills is not making payments to the right to disrespect or ill-treat you.

Day 273

It's not just about being in a relationship, it's about being in a happy and healthy one.

Day 274

Let's look at a divorce as an opportunity to get it right the next time.

Day 275

Doing the right thing is not always easy or popular but happiness is never about popularity.

Your family and friends like him because he is "good" with them. However, you are not happy with him. When you are alone with him, it's a nightmare. Unfortunately, they don't see that side of him; you do. They don't know your pain. So, what's a woman to do? Well, you aren't happy and you've tried to work it out numerous times so you think about leaving. Oh but wait, your family and friends love and adore him. If you tell them it's over they might blame you and some of them might not be happy with you for ending it. Remember, your happiness isn't about the popularity of your decision; it's about you. Sometimes you have to do what you have to do.

Day 276

If you are drifting apart, examine what held you together.

Day 277

If you're tired of trying to work things out start working your way out of the relationship.

Day 278

How he treats you is never determined by his looks.

Day 279

The man who loves you doesn't just say it; he shows it.

Day 280

Want the man who also wants you.

You can't have the man who doesn't want you. And sometimes, sadly, when he doesn't want you he plays games with you, creating false hope. Don't waste time wanting the man who doesn't want you. When you are wanted and needed, you know it. The man who wants and needs you will let you know by his actions.

Day 281

Too many lies breaks your trust in someone and if you can't trust them, it's difficult to be with them.

Day 282

Despite being in a relationship, you remain two different individuals but the relationship works because you want the same things.

Day 283

Your heart is precious and as a result you can't just give it to anyone. The person to whom you want to entrust your heart should demonstrate that they want it, will keep it, protect it and make it happy.

Day 284

His appearance could be part of your selection process but it shouldn't be the only one.

Day 285

One can speak many words yet say nothing while a single action can say it all.

Words can be empty and words can be powerful. Be careful, though, because some might speak powerful yet empty words. If a picture paints a thousand words, then actions paints a million: such is the power of actions. In a world where we require evidence and proof, words can't always be trusted. Many men can claim they love you, want to be with you and are committed to you but you must only believe the ones whose actions makes those claims true.

Day 286

True love is unconditional and transcends all biases and prejudices.

Day 287

Your perfect man is the man who's perfect for you.

Day 288

Dating is only a gamble if you don't know what you are looking for.

Day 289

Look for a man who will treat you as an equal, not as an inferior partner.

Day 290

If your heart is not in it, you're not in a real relationship.

A true relationship depicts two happy hearts, not one. Your heart has to be happy in your relationship. If your heart isn't into the relationship then you aren't in a real relationship. Whatever circumstances are responsible for your heart not being into the relationship, the fact of the matter is you aren't happy. Perhaps, you are probably just "existing" in the relationship, wanting to get out, wanting to change the situation. My advice is to follow your heart because your heart wants to lead you to happiness.

Day 291

The least popular women amongst men are the ones who have figured men out.

Day 292

The best man you can find is a man whose actions demonstrate he wants to be with you.

Day 293

Trust seals your relationship; when it is broken, it fills your relationship with insecurities.

Day 294

Sometimes a relationship wasn't meant to be; it involved no lies, no deception and no ulterior motives. It didn't work because it wasn't supposed to.

Day 295

There's no expiration date on leaving.

As long as you remain unhappy in your relationship, the option to leave does not expire. In fact, your relationship does not have to be an unhappy one – you can leave at any time. Sometimes you have to leave, particularly if it's a relationship plagued with unhappiness and un-fulfillment. You might feel trapped in a relationship for a variety of reasons but you should not forget that you can leave. Of course, leaving can sometimes be a difficult task, depending upon circumstances. However, if you are in an unhappy relationship, leaving, even if it's a last resort, does not have an expiration date.

Day 296

Hopefully you are in love and not infatuated; love is lasting, infatuation is fleeting.

Day 297

You will not always get it right but it's not an excuse to stop trying.

Day 298

When you allow men to easily slip into your life, they easily slip out.

Day 299

Tell me the truth so that I won't be led by your lies.

Day 300

Intimacy is part of the relationship; it's not the relationship.
Shoes makes walking comfortable, they don't make you walk. Having someone that you are intimate with doesn't mean you are in a relationship—unless of course if all you want is intimacy. Intimacy is only a part of a relationship because there are many other components to a relationship. Don't interpret being intimate as a sign of your being in a relationship particularly if the other components are missing. A relationship involves giving love and receiving love, appreciating and being appreciated, forgiving and compromising, caring and sharing, planning and growing together. Ask yourself, is it just intimacy or is it a relationship?

Day 301

If you keep having failed relationships then maybe you are not doing something right.

Day 302

A man hitting you once is once too many.

Day 303

You can't make him love you – he has to do that on his own.

Day 304

Don't be so blinded by words that you can't see actions.

Day 305

Bad relationships are parasitic, draining you mentally, emotionally, and physically.

Unhealthy and bad relationships are emotionally, mentally and physically draining. It is important that you seek to resolve such relationships— the sooner the better. A relationship should be the happy union of two people wanting to be in a relationship. Challenges are encountered in any relationship; however, prolonged unhealthy relationships – as defined by abuse of any kind, constant lying, cheating, selfishness, a lack of communication, taking your presence and contributions for granted, belittlement, or making one feel useless – should not be tolerated.

Day 306

Don't let the "ticking of your clock" rush you into making quick decisions about men. Entering into a relationship should not be based upon how much time you have but rather whether he's the man with the qualities you want.

Day 307

No more men on the rebound. Take that time to: cry, let go, improve and uplift yourself, love you more and make you a better you.

Day 308

Sometimes the best thing you can do is to give him some space.

Day 309

If you want your broken relationship to work, find out if he wants the same – you cannot fix it by yourself.

Day 310

When do you fight over a man who has brought another woman into your relationship? Never.

It's something I have great difficulty understanding. Your man brought another woman into your relationship. He probably didn't even tell her about you or if he did, he significantly downplayed your relationship or just lied about it. Still, you literally want to cut this other woman's head off. It's your man with whom you should be feuding and demanding to know why he brought another woman into the relationship. It is your man who is responsible. He should be explaining why he brought her into your lives.

Day 311

Loneliness can drive you in many directions. Don't let it drive you to regrettable places.

Day 312

Love shows.

Day 313

Single is a state of transition. Remain in that state for as long as it takes you to make the right transition out of it.

Day 314

Men who find you complicated are probably too simple for you anyway.

Day 315

Impatience with your single status maybe keeping you single.

If you are tired of being single and growing impatient with finding a man, then you might, in your quest or haste to find a man, make some mistakes. In fact, you will. If you are impatient, you might overlook red flags or ignore them. If you are impatient, you might see things you want to see and not what's actually there. If you are impatient, you could subconsciously via your words and actions convey this signal to a man. What this all means is that you might get into relationships but they would all be short-lived because you were in a rush and made mistakes. The likelihood of your impatience is that you'd spend more time being single than in a relationship.

Day 316

If most men just say what you want to hear, then you should judge a man based upon his actions.

Day 317

Sometimes you don't get the man you want, you get the man you need.

Day 318

One woman's trash could be another woman's treasure but sometimes trash is simply trash.

Day 319

If he wants to play games he should give you the option to decide for yourself if you want to play along.

Day 320

If love doesn't live there anymore neither should you.

In the beginning it was pure bliss. You couldn't get enough of each other – the laugher, dinners, special moments, etc... Now, it seems like you are virtual strangers, invading each other's space—space that was once not delineated. Perhaps the daily grind of life has taken a bite out of spontaneity and now all you have is mundane routines. Maybe you have tried to revive, to rejuvenate that love but it's all for naught. For whatever reason or reasons, you don't love him anymore or he doesn't love you. While I'm not happy to advocate leaving a relationship, sometimes it is precisely what is needed so that you or both of you can be happy again with someone else. If love doesn't live in the relationship anymore, why stay?

Day 321

He is not the one that got away... he simply was not the one.

Day 322

If your emotional needs and desires aren't met in your relationship, then you are emotionally lonely.

Day 323

Your relationship should not feel like you're in jail.

Day 324

If he doesn't have time for you maybe you're not worth his time – just a thought.

Day 325

A man must be deserving of you. Not all men are.

Most men pursue women. Naturally not all of these men who pursue you are worthy of you. Some women love the attention and other women think that because the man has shown some attention or interest, he's also worthy of some of hers. Nothing could be further from the truth. The men making catcalls to you in the street are showing you attention and interest. Sometimes, as a relationship progresses, you realize that perhaps a mistake was made—your mistake. He has changed. He's no longer the man to whom you were attracted. His actions and his treatment of you are in such contrast to your early dating days that you wonder how could you have been so wrong. Not all men are deserving of you. You should cautiously approach each relationship and really try to get to know the man. It will not be perfect but you can increase your chances of finding the man deserving of you.

Day 326

It is not enough to have him tell you he loves you, that's the easy part. He must show it.

Day 327

He must make you feel loved.

Day 328

The test of your relationship is what you both do in challenging moments.

Day 329

Soul mate – the person meant to be with you and for you, who transcends time and place, and overcomes obstacles. Against all odds, you end up together.

Day 330

One of the secrets to a beautiful and happy relationship is to ensure that your best friend, lover, confidante and partner are all the same person.

This is something you should try according to couples in healthy, long-lasting marriages and relationships. It is the secret to their success. It's awesome if you can freely confide in your partner who is also your best friend. It's euphoric if you can make love to your lover who is also your partner. Ignore people who talk about boredom in a relationship with the same person. You have at least four different ones to appreciate – lover, best friend, confidante and partner.

Day 331

Your relationship will last for as long as the both of you decide to keep it.

Day 332

You didn't want me then when I wanted you. You want me now when I don't want you – I've moved on.

Day 333

Boys play games; real men don't. Find you a real man.

Day 334

Who needs rules when you are in a relationship? In a true relationship, love makes the rules.

Day 335

Stop holding on to the man who has already left.

It could be that you really love him. He means so much to you; he has been there with you for so long, but now he is gone or going. If a man tells you he is leaving or he has left, you have to stop holding on to him. He's leaving for a reason; sadly, painfully, that reason is he no longer wants to be with you, whatever his reason(s). I know it's not easy to let go, particularly when you don't want to, but the reality is, if he is moving on or has moved on you should also do the same. Sometimes you have to pick up the pieces and start anew.

Day 336

You have to ensure your relationship needs are met.

Day 337

Relationships of substance are formed from a deep connection that is sometimes inexplicable to others and even to the two connected people themselves.

Day 338

Love is not about changing someone. Love is about accepting them for who they are since it is who they are that made you love them.

Day 339

Does he love you? Look at how he treats you.

Day 340

   A relationship should be a happy union of two people wanting to be with each other.

   Many people get into a relationship for a slew of wrong reasons. However, the ideal time and the ideal person is as stated in the above quote. Avoid frivolous reasons for getting into a relationship such as: you don't like being alone, all your friends have a man, your biological clock is ticking, etc... The objective is to be happy in your relationship, not just be in a relationship.

Day 341

The more time you spend in a bad relationship, the less time you have to get into a better one.

Day 342

It's okay to pursue a man; it's not okay to make a fool of yourself while doing so.

Day 343

Never set desperation standards for men.

Day 344

Divorce could be your pathway to happiness.

Day 345

The wedding does not make the marriage.

You probably dream of a grand wedding held at a spectacular location with breathtaking views and you probably want all of your guests to forever remember your wedding. Likewise, you want to be filled with pride and joy each time you look at your photos or review the video. Getting married at Sandals Beach Resorts on the island of Jamaica is no more a guarantee of a lasting marriage than another couple getting married in Las Vegas before an intoxicated priest. Your ultimate focus is on the marriage and the things you are both going to do and should do to make it a happy and lasting one.

Day 346

Marriage is not the end of your freedom. If you want freedom don't get married.

Day 347

A man should also be able to stimulate your mind.

Day 348

If you fall only for his looks you are superficial and superficial relationships don't last.

Day 349

Why be taken for granted, ignored, disrespected and unappreciated in a relationship when it won't happen if you are single?

Day 350

A relationship is not only about the treatment you receive, it is also about the treatment you give.

We should always try to be objective, impartial and fair. That we all have inherent biases and prejudices has never been doubted. However, we sometimes tend to see ourselves as perfect and without blame. We don't necessarily view ourselves this way from a pompous or prideful standpoint. Sometimes it's all subconscious, based on fear of our own dark side. In a relationship, in as much as you are concerned about the way your man treats you, you should be concerned or give thought to how you treat him. Treating your man the way you'd like to be treated is a great start. If you love him, let's hope complacency has not replaced your caring and concern for him. Are your actions demonstrative of your love for him? Do you show him and tell him he's appreciated? If you know in your heart that you treat him with love and respect, then you are truly being the ultimate partner to your man.

Day 351

You can't force a man to see how good you are... the right man will.

Day 352

Marriage should not signify the end of dating; continue to date your spouse.

Day 353

If he's not about you then maybe you shouldn't be about him.

Day 354

If all of your relationships have failed, maybe you've failed to have the most important one – a relationship with yourself. Spend time being single before the next one.

Day 355

At some point, his tricks become old; the trick is not to get old with them

Sometimes it's easy to know when he's lying to you. However, you are in love with him and you hope he will change. You've gotten used to all of his excuses and you find yourself, subconsciously, even making excuses for him to your family and friends. It's been months, years even, and has not changed. Yet there you are, still falling for the same old tricks and the same old excuses, but you are also getting older. Don't grow old with his tricks.

Day 356

He can only love you if it's in his heart to do so, which means you can't make him.

Day 357

If you are "trying" to make you happy in your relationship, perhaps you should try another relationship.

Day 358

It's not about who he is, it's about what he does.

Day 359

Persistent differences about what you both want in a relationship are an indication that you should both be with different people.

Day 360

Just as you gave a man the privilege of being with you, you can also take it away.

A man being with you is a privilege you have extended to him. He cannot be with you unless you agree. Sadly, it seems like some of you have forgotten about this power once you enter into the relationship. Some women put up with the most unacceptable behaviors exhibited by certain men. It is as if these women feel powerless, when the truth is they (you) have the power. He can't be with you unless you want him to be.

Day 361

The unchanged man tells you he has changed, the changed man shows you.

Day 362

Sexy is not all physical.

Day 363

It's not about the excitement of meeting someone new, it's about keeping the excitement new.

Day 364

You should remain single for as long as it takes you to find the right man for you.

Day 365

Love of self should be greater that love for a man.

When you love yourself you are able to give greater love. Love of self, means that you value you and that you care about you. Love of self means acting and being responsible. If you care about you, then you should do things that will not cause you pain or sorrow. You shouldn't accept treatment that you know you don't deserve and you shouldn't love another man more than you love yourself. You are very precious.

$\mathcal{BONUS}$ –

$\mathcal{Expansion}$ $\mathcal{Quotes:}$

It's not his looks; it's the man behind the looks.

It's hard to deny that physical attraction plays a role in many relationships. Something about him attracts you: facial features, his built, height, smile, etc... If you are looking for a serious relationship, it's not going to be based solely upon his looks; at least I hope not. Being handsome is one thing, how he treats you is way more important. A man's look is not all that defines him. He may look good but he may be unable to stimulate your mind and hold an intelligent conversation. He could be selfish, arrogant, mean-spirited and very uncaring. However, you won't know it if you are only focused on his looks. Hence, it's always a good idea to get to know him better and not be swayed by looks alone. You have to be able to look past his looks.

Why be taken for granted, ignored, disrespected and unappreciated in a relationship when it wouldn't happen if you were single?

There is great liberation in being single and sometimes you need to allow or let yourself be single. If you are in a relationship, supposedly with someone who loves you, they do not have the right to take you for granted, ignore or disrespect you. Sure they can but remember you can leave. Your relationship should be a happy one. If it's not then you have to take the initiative to make yourself happy. If you have repeatedly sought to rectify such a situation by initiating dialogue, forgiving him and trying different approaches but to no avail, then sometimes it's better being single.

The more chances you give him to get it right, the less chances you have of getting into the right relationship.

You should not spend most of the relationship giving him second chances, forgiving him or having him apologize to you. If you are spending a lot of time giving second chances, then you are giving yourself less and less time to be in a happy relationship. Clearly, the relationship isn't that great if you are always doing what the quote says. If you keep giving him more and more chances to get it right, then perhaps he's not the right man for you.

If he's not about you then maybe you shouldn't be about him.

I know, you really want him or you desperately want it to work and so you try and you try and you try to make it work. The key word here is "you." You are trying but he isn't or he isn't trying hard enough. You are all into him but by his actions—never mind what he says—he's not all into you. Do you know what is happening as you keep on trying? Time is passing you by and you become emotionally weary and vulnerable. There is someone out there who will be as much about you as you are about him.

If all of your relationships have failed, maybe you've failed to have the most important one – a relationship with yourself; spend time being single before the next one.

Avoid bouncing around from one relationship to another. Avoid using a new relationship to help you get over the last failed relationship. I'm not sure of the reasons why you keep having failed relationships but I do know what you should do between relationships. Instead of getting into a rebound relationship, it is best to reflect and try to understand why the relationship failed. Carefully analyze your actions, his actions and what you could and should have done differently. Take some time to revisit your expectations and don't be afraid to change, not lower, them, if you believe it's necessary. Spend more time with you before spending time with someone else.

When you invite a man into your life, it's to share it, not to take it over.

Unfortunately some men don't seem to understand this quote. Most importantly, you play a pivotal role in, if he doesn't understand it, making him understand that together you are both in a sharing relationship. Likewise, some women believe that a man who is domineering is just being a man. Unless you want a man dominating and taking over your life, not all men are like that. Obviously, if a man seeks to control your life, then you don't need him in your life. Seek a man who understands this quote.

You can't force a man to see how good you are… the right man will.

A man truly interested in you, a man who is with you for all the right reasons will see the good in you. In fact, he's probably with you because that's what attracted him to you. Such a man will appreciate those wonderful qualities that makes you the person you are. Good men recognize and appreciate your contributions to the relationship. They praise and acknowledge you so that you never have to doubt whether or not he is into you. If you find yourself having to remind him or if you have to find ways to draw his attention, then perhaps he's not the man for you. Why should you have to remind him of just how good you are to him? A good man won't forget how good you are.

Divorce could be your pathway to happiness.

No one, I hope, legitimately gets married to be divorced months or years later. We enter marriages with hope, glowing with love and great optimism for what the future holds. Marriage, like all relationships, has its challenges. There are moments of disagreements, moments to forgive and moments when the issuance of a heartfelt apology is needed. Marriage sometimes means making tough decisions but all for the betterment of the marriage and the growth of the couple.

Unfortunately, sometimes, despite our best and continued efforts (counseling, advice from friends, family, time away, additional compromise, sacrifices, etc…) to ride out or overcome those turbulent times in the marriage, nothing seems to work. When the marriage becomes a chore, when love no longer dwells, when conversations have disappeared and have been replaced by arguments or shouting matches, divorce could be your pathway to being happy once more.

Marriage should not signify the end of dating; continue to date your spouse.

Marriage should be a continuation of all the excitement of dating. That you are now married probably indicates you want to start or have started a family. If you have already done so, surely you have come to the realization that children demand a lot of your time. And if you intend to raise your children to become meaningful participants and contributors to society, then they become your priority.

However, becoming parents does not mean the end of your romance, the end of loving and caring for each other, the end of dating. Amidst the sometimes chaotic routine and patterns of life, find time for each other. Enjoy it all, enjoy each other, and enjoy your lifelong partner. Most of all, enjoy the love you feel for each other.

It's not about who he is, it's about what he does.

So, you are married to a doctor or you are dating a lawyer, ballplayer or someone society considers important. Career and profession aside, are you happy with him? Is he treating you like a man ought to treat a woman—particularly one he loves? Would you rather be treated with love, feel and receive love than be with a man who is important? It's not about how important he is, how famous or his great looks. When it comes to your relationship and your happiness in that relationship it's all about what he does and not about who he happens to be.

Marriage is not the end of your freedom. If you want freedom don't get married.

Some people talk about marriage as being the end of your freedom—a place of doom, a banishment to life with just one person. Such a description of marriage makes you wonder about the views those individuals have of dating. What is their take on a relationship leading up to marriage? Is it that they don't take dating seriously because you can always opt out? Is it that they see marriage as being more difficult to opt out of or they are not commitment material? If that is also your views of marriage then you are not the marrying type of individual and it would be best not to seek marriage.

A man should also be able to stimulate your mind.

Unless all you want to hear him talk about is sex, a man should be able to hold your interest with intellectually stimulating conversations. It's great to engage in conversations and have or share opinions on a variety of topics. Being able to talk about current events, hot topics and express one's self in a clear manner is a wonderful attribute. Have you ever tried having a conversation with someone who couldn't have a conversation? It's not a great experience.

I'm not implying that you should only look for college-educated men because there are some college-educated individuals that makes you want to check if they really did attend college. The point is that you should engage men in conversations, encourage them to talk. For it is in his conversations that you can tell a lot about the man.

The man you need in your life is the man who also needs you in his.

I get it. It can be downright difficult finding a man. However, though finding good men might be exhausting, finding the right man for you shouldn't be. The man you need in your life is the man who has demonstrated that he equally needs you in his. Beautiful promises and persuasive words are not demonstrative of a man's love or his desires to have you in his life. If he needs you in his life he's going to show you.

If your relationship becomes a drag, drag yourself out of it – quickly.

Life is short, too short. Relationships will have challenges and ideally both individuals should work together to amicably resolve those challenges. If the relationship, despite best efforts to resolve, becomes tiring and a drag then it's unhealthy. You should not spend most of your time trying to fix it. If you spend more time fixing rather than enjoying the relationship then it's time to get out of it. Relationships should not become burdensome and be emotional deadweight upon your heart.

Don't allow complacency to hitch a ride on your marital journey.

Being married is not a license to take your partner for granted. It's not an indication that you've "sealed the deal" so you can now focus exclusively on raising children and settling down to living life. Such an approach can and will quickly bring boredom, frustration and unhappiness into your marriage. As you journey through your marriage never take each other for granted. Don't stop doing the things you did before you got married.

It doesn't matter who said I love you first, it's a matter of who means it.

While there is a need, if you are looking for a committed relationship, to hear a man say I love you, there should be an even greater need for a man to show you that he loves you. It's okay if he says I love you first but you should not feel pressured to repeat those words back to him. Love is demonstrated and felt and only after being the recipient of such actions can you truly appreciate and believe those words as uttered. To believe love you must experience love.

www.ingramcontent.com/pod-product-compliance
Lightning Source LLC
Chambersburg PA
CBHW060929040426

42445CB00011B/860